Colo.) University Club (Denver, Colo.) (1892) bkp CU-BANC

University Club (Denver

The University Club

Colo.) University Club (Denver, Colo.) (1892) bkp CU-BANC University Club (Denver

The University Club

ISBN/EAN: 9783743306653

Manufactured in Europe, USA, Canada, Australia, Japa

Cover: Foto ©ninafisch / pixelio.de

Manufactured and distributed by brebook publishing software
(www.brebook.com)

Colo.) University Club (Denver, Colo.) (1892) bkp CU-BANC

University Club (Denver

The University Club

Directors, 1891

*CHARLES W. BADGLEY

WILLIAM R. BARBOUR

ALLAN M. CULVER

GEORGE Z. DIMMITT

CHARLES R. DUDLEY

EDWIN N. HAWKINS

JOHN L. JEROME

HERMAN C. JOY

HENRY F. MAY

OSCAR J. PFEIFFER

HENRY T. ROGERS

R. HEBER SMITH

CHARLES H. TOLL

*Elected March 19th, 1891, to fill vacancy caused by the
resignation of Lambert Sternbergh.

Officers, 1891

●

President
HENRY T. ROGERS

Vice-President
JOHN L. JEROME

Secretary
EDWIN N. HAWKINS

Treasurer
ALLAN M. CULVER
*HERMAN C. JOY

*Elected September 1st, 1891, to fill vacancy caused by the resignation of Allan M. Culver

Directors, 1891-1892

To serve until October, 1892

CHARLES W. BADGLEY

MOSES HALLETT

CHARLES J. HUGHES, JR.

JOHN L. JEROME

CHARLES H. TOLL

To serve until October, 1893

CHARLES R. DUDLEY

JEREMIAH T. ESKRIDGE

EDWIN N. HAWKINS

HENRY T. ROGERS

SAMUEL F. RATHVON

To serve until October, 1894

WILLIAM R. BARBOUR

HERMAN C. JOY

R. HEBER SMITH

JOEL F. VAILE

HENRY E. WOOD

Officers, 1891-1892

President
HENRY T. ROGERS

Vice-President
JOHN L. JEROME

Secretary
EDWIN N. HAWKINS

Treasurer
HERMAN C. JOY

Committees

1891-92

Executive Committee

CHARLES W. BADGLEY

WILLIAM R. BARBOUR

SAMUEL F. RATHVON

HENRY T. ROGERS

CHARLES H. TOLL

Committee on Literature and Art

CHARLES R. DUDLEY

R. HEBER SMITH

JOEL F. VAILE

Committees
1891-92

Committee on Admissions

To serve until October, 1892
J. TROWBRIDGE BAILEY
GEORGE Z. DIMMITT
SAMUEL A. FISK
JOHN L. JEROME, Chairman
HENRY F. MAY

To serve until October, 1893
LUCIUS M. CUTHBERT
CHARLES R. DUDLEY
LEIGHTON HOWARD-SMITH
BYRON C. LEAVITT
EDWARD B. MORGAN

To serve until October, 1894
ALLAN M. CULVER
THOMAS H. HARDCASTLE, Secretary
ALBERT E. PATTISON
HENRY T. ROGERS
THOMAS B. STEARNS

Articles of Incorporation

of

The University Club

Know all men by these presents, That we, John L. Jerome, William R. Barbour, George Z. Dimmitt, Henry F. May, Henry T. Rogers, R. Heber Smith, Lambert Sternbergh, Allan M. Culver, Charles H. Toll, Charles R. Dudley, and Edwin N. Hawkins, all residents of the City of Denver and State of Colorado, and citizens of the United States, being desirous of associating ourselves for social purposes and not for pecuniary profit, and by virtue and in pursuance of the provisions of Chapter 19 of the General Statutes of Colorado, and the acts amendatory thereof and supplementary thereto, do hereby associate ourselves together as a body corporate, and we do hereby make, execute and acknowledge this our certificate in writing of our intention to so become a body corporate, not for pecuniary profit, and therefore state and set forth :

First—The corporate name of our said association and corporation shall be THE UNIVERSITY CLUB.

Second—The objects for which our said association is formed, shall be to promote social intercourse among ourselves and associates in said Club, the encouragement of literature and art, and the establishment and maintenance of a library, reading-room and club house for the use of ourselves and associates, with all the appurtenances, belongings, matters and things usual or desirable in connection therewith.

Third—The number of directors to manage the said Club or association shall be thirteen ; but the members of said Club shall have power to increase the number of the directors, if at any time they desire so to do, in the manner prescribed by the Constitution or By-laws of the Club.

Fourth—The following are the names of the directors of such Club or Association for the first year of its existence, to-wit : Charles H. Toll, John L. Jerome, Charles R. Dudley, Herman C. Joy, R. Heber Smith, William R. Barbour, Oscar J. Pfeiffer, Lambert Sternbergh, Edwin N. Hawkins, Henry T. Rogers, Allan M. Culver, Henry F. May, and George Z. Dimmitt.

Fifth — The principal operations of said Club shall be carried on in the City of Denver, County of Arapahoe, and State of Colorado, and the Club House shall be maintained in said City.

Sixth—The directors of said Club or association shall have power, from time to time, to made such prudential by-laws as they shall deem proper for the management of the affairs of said Club, and for the government and management of its business, and for the qualifications and conduct of its members.

In witness whereof, We have to this certificate respectively signed our names on this, the twenty-ninth day of January, A. D. 1891.

> JOHN L. JEROME
> WILLIAM R. BARBOUR
> GEORGE Z. DIMMITT
> HENRY F. MAY
> HENRY T. ROGERS
> R. HEBER SMITH
> LAMBERT STERNBERGH
> ALLAN M. CULVER
> CHARLES H. TOLL
> CHARLES R. DUDLEY
> EDWIN N. HAWKINS

The foregoing certificate was acknowledged January 29, 1891, and filed in the office of the Secretary of State January 31, 1891.

Constitution

•

ARTICLE I

Name

The name of this association is THE UNIVERSITY CLUB.

ARTICLE II

Officers

The officers of the Club shall be a President, Vice-President, Secretary and Treasurer.

ARTICLE III

Duties of Officers

Section 1—President.—The President, or, in his absence, the Vice-President, shall preside at the meetings of the Club and of the Board of Directors. In the event of their absence, the Club or Board of Directors may elect its presiding officer. The President shall sign all written contracts and obligations of the Club, and shall perform such other duties as the Board of Directors or the Club may assign him.

Sec. 2 — Treasurer. — The Treasurer shall collect all admission fees and all dues, and shall keep the accounts of the Club and report thereon at each regular meeting of the Board of Directors. He shall pay all bills on the certificate of their correctness by the Executive Committee.

Sec. 3 — Secretary. — The Secretary shall give notice of all meetings of the Club and of the Board of Directors, and shall keep minutes of such meetings. He shall conduct the correspondence and keep the records of the Club. He shall notify persons elected to membership of their election, and shall be the keeper of the corporate seal of the Club.

Sec. 4 — Vice-President. — In the case of the absence, resignation, death or removal from office of the President, the Vice-President shall perform all duties pertaining to the office of President during the continuance of such absence or vacancy.

ARTICLE IV

Meetings of the Club

Section 1.—There shall be an annual meeting of the Club at the Club house, on the last Wednesday of October in each year, at 8 o'clock P. M.

Sec. 2.—Forty resident members shall constitute a quorum at all Club meetings. If there be no quorum before the hour of nine o'clock, the presiding officer shall adjourn the meeting from time to time until a quorum shall be had, and notice of every such adjournment shall be given as hereinafter provided for service of notice.

Sec. 3—Order of Business.—

1. Roll Call
2. Reading of the minutes of last meeting
3. Reports of Officers
4. Reports of Committees
5. General Business
6. Election of Officers

Sec. 4—Election of Officers.— At the annual meeting of the Club to be held on the last Wednesday of October, 1891, the Club shall ballot for fifteen directors, and the directors so elected shall divide themselves by lot into three classes of five members each ; one of such classes shall hold office for three years, one for two years, and the third for one year ; and at each annual meeting thererafter the Club shall ballot for five directors to take the place of the outgoing class. Vacancies occurring in the Board of Directors shall be temporarily filled by a vote of the Board; but at the next annual meeting after the occurrence of such vacancy, a director shall be elected to serve the unexpired portion of such term.

Sec. 5—Special Meetings.—Upon the written request of twenty-five members of the Club, the Directors shall call a special meeting of the Club; such request, as well as the notice of the meeting, shall state the objects for which the meeting is called, and at a special meeting, no subject not so stated shall be considered. Notices of any meeting, whether annual or special, shall be posted in the rooms of the Club for at least one week preceding the meeting, and a notice in writing shall also be sent to each resident member of the Club at least ten days preceding the meeting. Special meetings may also be called at any time by order of the Board of Directors.

ARTICLE V

Board of Directors

Section 1. — The Board of Directors shall have general charge of the affairs, funds, and property of the Club; they shall have full power, and it shall be their duty, to carry out the purposes of the Club according to its charter, constitution and by-laws.

Sec. 2.—The Board of Directors shall, as soon as may be after each annual meeting, elect from its own body a President, Vice-President, Secretary and Treasurer, who shall hold office until the next annual election, and until their successors are elected.

Sec. 3.—The Board of Directors shall submit, at each annual meeting, a general report of the affairs of the Club, with an estimate for the ensuing year, which shall be printed and distributed to the members five days before the annual meeting, and the Board of Directors shall report at other times if required.

Sec. 4.—The Board of Directors shall meet once a month, and special meetings may be called by order of the President or of any three Directors. A majority of the members of the Board shall constitute a quorum.

Sec. 5.—The Board of Directors shall prescribe the rules for the admission of strangers to the privileges of the Club.

Sec. 6.—The Board of Directors may fill any vacancy in its body by election of a member to hold office until the next annual election.

Sec. 7.—The Board of Directors shall have power to remit penalties for offenses against the rules, and for unintentional violations of the constitution.

ARTICLE VI

Qualification of Members

Section 1.—Any man shall be eligible to membership in this Club, who has received from a University or College a degree, to obtain which, in regular course, at least two years' residence and study are required, or who shall have received an honorary degree from such University or College, or who shall have graduated at the United States Military Academy, or at the United States Naval Academy ; provided that a candidate who holds an honorary degree only shall be distinguished in art, literature, science, or the public service ; and provided that professional degrees shall entitle to membership only when given by such University or College as shall be designated by the Board of Directors, and the list of such Universities and Colleges shall be posted in the rooms of the Club.

Sec. 2.—The Board of Directors shall determine what degrees from what foreign Universities shall qualify holders thereof for membership.

ARTICLE VII

Committee on Admissions

Section 1.—Prior to the annual meeting of the Club, to be held on the last Wednesday in October, 1891, the Board of Directors shall act as the Committee on Admissions, and be governed by the rules hereinafter prescribed for the government of the Committee on Admissions.

Sec. 2.—At the meeting of the Club held on the last Wednesday in October, 1891, there shall be elected a committee of fifteen, who shall be known as the Committee on Admissions. Such committee, immediately after its election, shall divide itself by lot into three classes of five each, one of which classes shall serve for three years, one for two years, and the third for one year. At each annual election thereafter, five members of the Club shall be elected to take the place of the outgoing class, and to serve for three years on the Committee on Admissions. Vacancies arising during the year may be filled by the Committee, but at each annual election members shall be elected by ballot of the Club to fill such vacancies.

Sec. 3.—Eight members of the Committee shall constitute a quorum, and all candidates for admission shall be voted for by ballot, and two negative votes shall be a rejection of the candidate. The names of the Committee shall remain posted in a conspicuous place in the Club rooms. The name, residence and college, or place of instruction, and the date of the degree of every person proposed for admission, with the names of the members proposing and seconding, shall be exposed in a conspicuous place in the Club house for at least two weeks. The matter shall then be referred to the Committee on Admissions. The proceedings of the Committee shall be secret and confidential. It shall be the duty of the Committee, after careful consideration and examination, to vote upon each name separately.

ARTICLE VIII

Membership

Section 1.—The resident membership of the Club shall be limited to two hundred.

Sec. 2.—Not to exceed five life members may be admitted, or qualified from the present membership, upon payment of a membership fee of five hundred dollars. Such members shall have all the privileges of resident members and be exempt from the payment of annual dues.

ARTICLE IX

Resignations

Section 1.— Resignations of memberships shall be made to the Secretary in writing, and no resignation shall be accepted unless the member presenting it has paid all current indebtedness to the Club, including the dues for the quarter during which said resignation takes effect.

ARTICLE X

Dues

Section 1.—The admission fee shall be fifty dollars for resident members, and twenty-five dollars for non-resident members ; but every non-resident member who shall become a resident member shall pay to the Treasurer an amount equal to the difference between his original admission fee, and the admission fee for resident members at the time of his admission as a non-resident member ; and a failure to pay said sum shall be considered a failure to pay dues, and shall subject the member to the penalties prescribed for the failure to pay dues.

Sec. 2.—The annual dues of resident members shall be fifty dollars, and of non-resident members twenty-five dollars, payable quarterly in advance.

Sec. 3.— A person not residing or having a place of business within ten miles of the Club house, may be elected a non-resident member, and any member who removes his residence or place of business a distance of not less than ten miles from the Club house, on written notice to the Treasurer shall become a non-resident member.

Sec. 4.—Non-resident members shall not be entitled to vote at any meeting of the Club or to hold any office.

Sec. 5.—Candidates elected, on payment of the admission fee and of the dues of the current quarter, shall become members of the Club, and the election of any candidate shall be void if he fail to make such payment within thirty days after notice of his election is mailed, addressed to him at the place given as his residence on the posted list of candidates.

Sec. 6.—Should the dues of any member remain unpaid for the space of one month, the Treasurer shall notify him in writing that unless his dues are paid within one month from the date of such notice, his membership shall cease ; and unless such dues are paid pursuant to such notice, or such default is accounted for to the satisfaction of the Board of Directors, he shall thereupon cease to be a member of the Club.

Sec. 7.— In case of absence of any

resident member of the Club for a period of six consecutive months or more, the Board of Directors may make such remission of dues in his favor as they may think proper.

ARTICLE XI
Discipline

Section 1.—Any member may be suspended, expelled or reprimanded for cause, by a vote of two-thirds of all the members of the Board of Directors; provided, that before any member of the Club is disciplined by the Board of Directors he shall be entitled to at least one week's notice, in writing, of the charges preferred against him, the time and place when the meeting of the Board will be held to consider the same, and shall be given an opportunity to present any defense which he may have at such meeting of the Board.

Sec. 2.—The Board of Directors shall have full authority to discipline any member in the manner above provided, for conduct deemed by the Board detrimental to the welfare, interests or character of the Club.

Sec. 3.— At any time within thirty days after a sentence of expulsion, a meeting of the Club to consider the same shall be called, if a written request be made by twelve members thereof to the President. At such meeting an appeal may be taken from the decision of the Board of Directors, and the member expelled may be restored by a vote of a majority of the members present.

ARTICLE XII

Rules

Section 1.—The Board of Directors shall prepare and enforce rules regulating the use of the Club rooms.

Sec. 2.—The Board of Directors and Committee on Admissions shall each have power to make rules for its government, and to prescribe and enforce penalties for the violation of such rules.

ARTICLE XIII

Appointment of Committees

The Board of Directors shall appoint from its own members an Executive Committee and a Committee on Literature and Art, to be standing committees for the current year. The first Board of Directors shall also appoint a Membership Committee of five persons, who shall consider all applications for membership and report the same to the Board.

ARTICLE XIV

Executive Committee

The Executive Committee shall make all purchases authorized by the Board; regulate the price to be charged upon all articles to be served in the Club; report the names of such members as are in arrears, and the sums they respectively owe; appoint such sub-committees as they may deem proper; employ and discharge servants, and have a general supervision of the internal economy and regulation of the Club.

ARTICLE XV

Committee on Literature and Art

This committee, under the direction of the Board of Directors, shall have charge of the reading-room, and of all books and works of art belonging to the Club, and shall have power to solicit donations and select and purchase books, periodicals and works of art for the Club.

ARTICLE XVI

Notice to Members

Any member may enter in a book to be kept at the office, a mail address, to which all notices to be sent to him under the Constitution or Rules shall be directed. In default of such entry, notices shall be served by depositing them in the Club letter box, addressed to the member, who shall be held to have received them one week after they shall have been so mailed or deposited.

ARTICLE XVII

Amendments

The Constitution may be amended at any meeting of the Club by a vote of a majority. Notices of proposed amendments shall be furnished to the Secretary and posted in the Club house at least twenty days before the meeting at which it is proposed to consider them, and the Secretary shall cause such notices to be printed and sent to each member, at least ten days before such meeting.

Rules for the Government

of the

Board of Directors

●

Meetings

1.—The regular monthly meeting of the Board shall be held on the first Tuesday of each month, at 8 o'clock P. M.

Officers

2.—At the first meeting of the Board following the annual meeting of the Club, the officers provided for by the Constitution shall be elected by ballot.

Proceedings

3.—The proceedings, actions and deliberations of the Board shall be considered secret, and shall not be discussed with any person outside the Board.

4.—The ayes and noes on any motion before the Board shall be called and recorded by the Secretary at the request of any two members, and such call shall be in order at any time before any other motion shall be made.

Fines

5.—A fine of one dollar shall be levied upon every member who shall not be present within fifteen minutes after the hour appointed for any regular or special meeting; but such fine may be remitted by the Board for good cause shown.

Committees

6.—The Board shall, at its first meeting, appoint an Executive Committee, consisting of five members, of which the President shall be one; also a Committee on Literature and Art, consisting of three members.

Rules

7.—These rules may be amended or added to at any meeting of the Board, by a vote of two-thirds of the Board.

Extracts from the Rules

for the Government of the

Committee on Admissions

●

Meetings of the Committee

5.—A stated meeting of the Committee shall be held on the first Tuesday of each month, at 8 o'clock P. M.

6.—Special meetings of the Committee shall be called by the Secretary, on the direction of the Chairman, or the written request of three members of the Committee.

Candidates for Admission

11.—Every proposer of a candidate shall state in his formal proposal the college at which the candidate graduated, the degree obtained by him, the year in which he received such degree, his residence, and his profession or occupation. If he have no occupation, that fact shall be stated. Upon the receipt by the Secretary of such formal proposal, duly signed by one member of the Club as proposer, and by one or more members of the Club as seconders, the name, college, degree, date of graduation and residence of the candidate, shall be exposed in a conspicuous place in the Club house for at least two weeks; after the expiration of which time, but not before, the name of the candidate may be called up for consideration by the Committee.

12.—Every proposer of a candidate is required to send to the Committee on Admissions, in addition to his formal proposal, a letter of recommendation stating the facts required to be stated in the formal proposal, and also such statement of the qualifications of the candidate as the proposer may deem proper. Letters of recommendation are also required from all persons seconding the nomination of candidates. Any member of the Club may also send to the Committee a letter stating such facts, with reference to any candidate, as he may deem proper for the consideration of the Committee. All letters to the Committee shall be considered by them as strictly confidential, and the contents thereof shall not be communicated to any person not a member of the Committee. If the name of a candidate is called up for consideration by the Committee and it shall then appear that the proposer or any of the seconders of such candidate has failed to send a letter of recommendation, as required by this rule, the name of the candidate shall be passed, and the Secretary shall at once notify the proposer and all seconders of such candidate who have failed to send such letters, that the nomination cannot be acted upon without a compliance with this rule. In case this rule has not been fully complied with before the next following stated meeting, the candidate shall be deemed withdrawn, his name dropped from the list, and his proposer and seconders notified of the fact.

13.—The name of a candidate for non-resident membership shall not be considered by the Committee, unless a letter respecting his candidacy shall have been received from a resident member of the Club, or unless such candidate shall be personally known to some member of the Committee present at the time when the name of such candidate shall be called up for consideration.

14.—Letters, except those of the proposer and seconders, relating to candidates whose names have been finally acted upon, shall forthwith be destroyed, unless by a vote of the Committee the Secretary be directed to preserve any particular letter or letters.

15.—Candidates for resident membership must be personally known to at least one member of the Committee present at the time their names shall be called up for consideration. If no member of the Committee present at such time is personally acquainted with the candidate, the name of the candidate shall be passed.

House Rules

•

Hours

The Club House will be open every day from seven (7) A. M.

The wine room will be closed at midnight, and no member except lodgers will be admitted to the Club House after that hour.

Restrictions

No member, guest or visitor, shall give any money or gratuity to the servants of the Club.

Members shall not take from the Club House any article belonging to the Club.

No subscription paper shall be circulated, nor any article exposed for sale in the Club House, without the authority of the Executive Committee.

No member shall use a billiard table for more than three consecutive games, to the exclusion of others desiring to play.

Any glassware or other property of the Club broken or injured by any member, shall be paid for by him.

Notices shall not be posted on the bulletin board, except upon the authority or approval of the Executive Committee.

No picture or decoration shall be placed in the Club House, except with the approval of the Committee on Literature and Art.

No member of the Club shall be permitted to send any employe out of the Club House for any purpose, or to call upon him for any service that takes him away from his duties at the Club House.

Games

Betting in the Club House will be restricted to twenty-five (25) cents per rubber point at whist, and ten (10) cents per heart in the game of hearts.

No other game for a wager of more than twenty-five (25) cents per game will be allowed.

Poker and other well-known gambling games are positively prohibited. Any violation of this rule will render the offending member liable to suspension.

Complaints

Complaints or suggestions must be addressed to the Board of Directors, and signed by the member making the same. They may be delivered to the Steward, or deposited in the box provided for that purpose in the office of the Club.

Indebtedness

Members are requested to sign cards for all orders.

A statement of the account of each member will be rendered on the last day of each month, and if not paid by the fifteenth of the following month, the name of the member whose account is then unpaid and the amount of his indebtedness, will be posted on the bulletin board until paid.

If any member who is posted for an indebtedness does not discharge the same on or before the first day of the following month, he will have no further credit extended to him, until such account shall have been paid.

Steward's Report

The Steward is instructed to report to the Board of Directors at each meeting, the names of any members of the Club who have violated any of the rules or regulations of the Club. He shall also report the names of any members whose accounts are in arrears.

Privileges of Club House

A member may invite a stranger to the use of the Club House for one day, by recording his name upon the visitors' book, but can have no more than two guests at a time.

Upon the request of a member, and the written assent of a member of the

Board of Directors, a card of invitation will be issued to a stranger for two weeks, and such invitation may be repeated if the stranger has been absent from the city for three months. The invitation to a stranger may be extended beyond two weeks, for a period not exceeding sixty days, upon payment of a fee of five dollars ($5) for each two weeks.

No invitation can be extended beyond sixty days except upon the order of the Board of Directors.

The Board of Directors may revoke any invitation at any time.

The names and places of residence of strangers, and the names of the members inviting them, must be recorded, and hosts are held responsible for their guests.

List of Members

•

Resident Members

BADGLEY, CHARLES W.,
1805 Market Street

BAILEY, J. TROWBRIDGE,
Boston Building

BARBOUR, WILLIAM R.,
Colorado National Bank Building

BARTELS, GUSTAVE C.,
People's National Bank Building

BARTELS, LOUIS F.,
813 Seventeenth Street

BERGER, GEORGE B.,
Colorado National Bank

BLOOD, JAMES H.,
People's National Bank Building

BOAL, THEODORE H.,
Jacobson Building

BRYANT, WILLIAM H.,
Ernest-Cranmer Building

CATTANACH, ANDREW J.,
701 Fourteenth Street

CHANUTE, ARTHUR,
Globe Smelting and Refining Co.

CHURCH, FRANK,
American National Bank

COOPER, JOB A.,
National Bank of Commerce

COOVER, DAVID H.,
Kittredge Building

COY, NATHAN B.,
Barclay Building

CRAIG, WILLIAM BAYARD,
57 South Broadway

CULVER, ALLAN M.,
1742 Curtis Street

CUTHBERT, LUCIUS M.,
Boston Building

DAVIS, J. CULVER,
1628 Lincoln Avenue

DAYTON, WILLIAM L.,
Good Block

DENISON, JOHN H.,
Patterson & Thomas Block

DIMMITT, GEORGE Z.,
Ernest-Cranmer Building

DIXON, EDWARD L.,
Duff Block

DUDLEY, CHARLES R.,
Mercantile Library

ELLIS, DANIEL B.,
Boston Building

ESKRIDGE, JEREMIAH T.,
Barth Block

EVANS, HOWARD,
American National Bank

FISK, SAMUEL A.,
37 Eighteenth Avenue

FLEMING, JOHN D.,
37 Gettysburg Building

FURMAN, H. VAN F.,
1526 High Street

GOVE, AARON,
2045 Grant Avenue

GRANT, JAMES B.,
1280 Grant Avenue

GREENE, J. SIRE,
Barclay Building

HALE, IRVING,
537 Sixteenth Street

HALLETT, MOSES,
U. S. District Court

HARDCASTLE, THOMAS H..
Ernest-Cranmer Building

HAWKINS, EDWIN N.,
Globe Smelting and Refining Co.

HAWKINS, J. DAWSON,
Globe Smelting and Refining Co.

HELM, JOSEPH C.,
Barclay Building

HERR, WILLIS B.,
1646 Arapahoe Street

HERSHEY, EDWIN P.,
1045 South Fifteenth Street

HILL, CRAWFORD,
Boston Building

HILL, NATHANIEL P.,
Boston Building

HOBSON, HENRY W.,
Ernest-Cranmer Building

HOWARD-SMITH, LEIGHTON,
1632 California Street

HUDSON, GRANT L.,
1622 Arapahoe Street

HUGHES, JR., CHARLES J.,
Hughes Block

ILES, MALVERN W.,
Globe Smelting and Refining Co.

JEROME, JOHN L.,
Colorado National Bank Building

JOHNSON, EDWARD L.,
Symes Block

JOHNSON, HENRY V.,
Ernest-Cranmer Building

JOY, HERMAN C.,
1310 Eighteenth Street

KESTNER, CHRISTIAN C.,
University Club

LEAVITT, BYRON C.,
1517 Stout Street

LYMAN, CHARLES B.,
1517 Stout Street

LYNE, HENRY,
Globe Smelting and Refining Co.

MAGUIRE, WILLIAM M.,
Clayton Block

MAIN, JOHN F.,
721 Seventeenth Street

MANLY, GEORGE C.,
Ernest-Cranmer Building

MAY, HENRY F.,
Cheesman Block

MILLER, HENRY S.,
Lennox Chambers, 1737 California Street

MORGAN, EDWARD B.,
Patterson & Thomas Block

MORRIS, NORMAN K.,
Denver Club

PARMELEE, HARLAN P.,
Cheesman Block

PATTISON, ALBERT E.,
Charles Building

PEARCE, HAROLD V.,
1712 Sherman Avenue

PEARCE, RICHARD,
1712 Sherman Avenue

PFEIFFER, OSCAR J.,
Barth Block

PUGH, MARSHALL R.,
1702 Champa Street

RATHVON, SAMUEL F.,
Boston Building

RAYMOND, WILBUR S.,
Sixteenth Avenue, corner Race Street

RIVERS, EDMUND C.,
Bancroft Building

ROGERS, HENRY T.,
Boston Building

ROLLINS, EDWARD W.,
Ernest-Cranmer Building

RUST, GEORGE,

Tabor Block

SHAFROTH, JOHN F.,

Tabor Block

SLEEPER, JOHN W.,

Cheesman Block

SMITH, EDWARD H.,

1742 Curtis Street

SMITH, R. HEBER,

Patterson & Thomas Block

SMITH, WILLIAM BUZARD,

Ernest-Cranmer Building

STEARNS, THOMAS B.,

1720 California Street

STEARNS, JR., JOEL W.,

Duff Block

STEDMAN, ARNOLD,

1405 Welton Street

STERNBERGH, LAMBERT,

Redlands, California

TALBOT, RALPH,

Patterson & Thomas Block

TEBBETTS, JOHN S.,

Denver Club

TEBBETTS, WILLIAM B.,

Symes Block

THOMAS, CHARLES S.,

Ernest-Cranmer Building

TOLL, CHARLES H.,

Colorado National Bank Building

TUCKER, JOHN H.,

Globe Smelting and Refining Co.

VAILE, JOEL F.,

                  Cheesman Block

VROOM, J. NICOLL,

                  Mack Building

WADLEIGH, FRANK A.,

                  Cheesman Block

WAGNER, HENRY R.,

                  University Club

WEST, DE WITT C.,

                  1811 Grant Avenue

WOLCOTT, EDWARD O.,

                  Cheesman Block

WOOD, HENRY E.,

                  1742 Arapahoe Street

WOODWARD, FRANK L.,

                  1617 Lawrence Street

WRIGHT, FRANK H.,

                  1510 Arapahoe Street

Non-Resident Members

ABBOTT, JAMES W.,
Ouray

BAKER, JAMES H.,
Boulder

CRAGG, SAMUEL W.,
Gold Hill

DEVEREUX, HORACE K.,
Aspen

DEVEREUX, WALTER B.,
Glenwood Springs

DUNHAM, MAURICE E.,
Boulder

EDSALL, THOMAS H.,
Colorado Springs

EHRICH, LOUIS R.,
Colorado Springs

GAST, CHARLES E.,
Pueblo

HAGERMAN, JAMES J.,
Colorado Springs

HAGERMAN, PERCY,
Colorado Springs

JAMES, SAMUEL,
Pioche, Nevada

LAMBERT, EDWARD W.,
2 East 37th St., New York City

LOCKE, BRADFORD H.,
Central City

LUNT, HORACE G.,
Colorado Springs

McINTIRE, ALBERT W.,
La Jara

MATHEZ, AUGUSTE,
Black Hawk

NEWBERRY, WOLCOTT E.,
Aspen

PALMER, CORTLANDT E.,
Aspen

ROGERS, EDWARD M.,
Aspen

SLOCUM, JR., WILLIAM F.,
Colorado Springs

STIMSON, EDWARD C.,
Aspen

TAYLOR, FRANK M.,
Aspen

WILSON, CHARLES S.,
Aspen

WILSON, JR., HENRY M.,
Pueblo

•